Ah sweet misunderstandings
That allow us to embrace
Incompatible truths

—Michael Joseph

The Hobo's Crowbar

JonArno Lawson
woodcuts by Alec Dempster

The Porcupine's Quill

Library and Archives Canada Cataloguing in Publication

Lawson, JonArno, author
  The hobo's crowbar/JonArno Lawson;wood engravings by
Alec Dempster.

Poems.
ISBN 978-0-88984-399-8 (paperback)

  I. Children's poetry, Canadian (English). I. Dempster, Alec,
1971–, illustrator II. Title.

PS8573.A93H63 2016   jc811'.54   c2016-904333-9

Published by The Porcupine's Quill, 68 Main Street, PO Box 160,
Erin, Ontario NOB 1TO. http://porcupinesquill.ca

Represented in Canada by Canadian Manda Group.
Trade orders are available from University of Toronto Press.

We acknowledge the support of the Ontario Arts Council and the
Canada Council for the Arts for our publishing program. The
financial support of the Government of Canada through the
Canada Book Fund is also gratefully acknowledged.

Remembering my old friend
John Cosby Day
(1968–2015)

and my new friend
Iain Marrs
(1956–2015)

was riding along
on the silence bicycle
fell off again: spoke

—Iain Marrs

The Hobo's
CROWBAR

Hobo's Crowbar

With a beggar's bowl
You can only go so far—
Skip out and hop it
With a hobo's crowbar.

Not Just Anybody Can Become a Somebody

For a Nobody to become a Somebody
Somebody has to notice
The Nobody—
It can't be just Anybody—

(and if Nobody notices Somebody
that doesn't matter to Anybody at all).

It's when Somebody
Notices the Nobody
That the Nobody's chance
To become a Somebody

Becomes as good as Anybody's.

What Can't Be Learned from Experience

In time you will learn
from experience
what you can't learn
from experience.

Vigilantes with Good Intentions Perform Required Interventions

Drunken uncles
frantic aunties
Rankle clear-eyed
vigilantes

Drunken uncles
Roll the dice
Frantic aunties
Pay the price

Vigilantes give advice:
While uncles stroll around the mall
Aunties—dump their alcohol!

Grumpy uncles
Grateful aunties
Glare and glint at
vigilantes

Spunky Dunker

There was a spunky dunker who swept across the flux
she floated in the flotsam
and trudgened in her tux

Shouts from the shore
Had her turning about
where wrathful officers hollered her out

Her peace was disturbed
So as smooth as a trout
She disappeared under the ducks.

Blast It, Betty!

Blast it, Betty—
What the heck?!
Get your elbow
Off my neck!
Don't you ever think to check?
You're the reason I'm a wreck!
Drowning out my ZANG with dreck!

Dash it all, and darn it—drat!
Wheredja put my cowboy hat?
Whydja go and squash it flat?
Gitcher offit—scatcha cat
Woman zipzap—man kersplat!

Betty! *It's as bad as that!*

Nuts to you, Bet—
Rats! Kaput!
Doe-see-doe-ing
On my foot!
Zut alors!
Nicht sehr gut!

Execrate!
Anathematize!
Objurgate,
chide and chastise!

Shucks and golly!
Curse your eyes!
Bust your blather—
Blast your lies!

Under a Billboard at Bathurst and Eglinton

Under a billboard at Bathurst and Eglinton
Using nothing but my eyes
I bought some clouds—
Because they were big and self-sufficient

but I bought them too for protection—
Since a friend of mine
Once safely walked this same street
under similar clouds

They passed over the same sidewalks she passed over
But the past can't be touched, and you can't touch clouds
And there's something wrong inside me
and the clouds might solve it ...

I bought them also because they're grey without being depressing—
And slow, but not in a way that makes me impatient
Because having nowhere to be or go
Doesn't stop them from being or going

They travel like jokes
So I accept them as natural
See how they activate my wit
without taking credit

Because they ask nothing
And pull me gently away from
the great loneliness
to which no one gets accustomed

but the clouds.

You'll Learn Not to Mind

You'll learn not to mind
Your mind if you're smart—
And if you have a heart
Then you'll take things to heart.

How to Get to the Future

You get
there
just by
being here

How to Get to the Past

You get
there
just by
being here

Human Nature

There's something you can't afford to neglect—
Human nature!—
It's worth the study—
Because one thing you can't ever expect
Is anything
From anybody.

The Energy of Anarchy

The energy of anarchy is agony
The energy of anarchy is brief
The agony will take you to the border
Of the order that exists beyond belief.

You've Tried Too Hard to Love

You've tried too hard to love, my love
And now (my love) it's time
To close your open mind
And leave your love behind.

Exits Exist

Exits exist
Entrances too
Look and you'll find them
In all that you do

The Bald Man's Store

The bald man's store
sold a tonic
to help the balding grow new hair—
How ironic!

I asked the bald man
if he planned to try it—
he said, 'Son,
I sell it—but I don't buy it.'

Regal O'Reilly

To really rally O'Reilly
They resorted to clamorous clapping—
Regal O'Reilly took offence:
'Applause without cause doesn't make any sense,
kindly suppress this unruly pretense—
cease at once, please,'
O'Reilly said drily.

Seize Her Caesar

Caesar sees her …
'Seize her, Caesar!
Caesar!
Caesar?'

Caesar seizes her
then frees her—
She knees Caesar—
Caesar flees her.

28

How Long Will It Last?

I look down my nose at the past
Like a spoiled domestic cat—
Like the cat I know that the present will last
Long enough for that.

The Big Guy Says Goodnight

The bright moon moves slowly
through the
black sky

low-down
and slow-moving moving
up high

The far-away moves slowly till it's
nearby
Goodnight, sweet dreams, goodnight.

The hello rolls over on the
goodbye
The left eye looks over at the

right eye
The small fry is staring at the
big guy

The big guy says goodnight.

There's Something Almost Real

There's something almost real
In everything that's fake
Like some banana peel
That startles you awake
It gets beneath your heel
You slip out of your trance
And fall and crack your head
On stones meant for your feet
And if you crawl away enlightened
Then your journey is complete.

Some Hitches in the Expanding Sense of a Global Human Family

Their lives may be miserable,
cruel and foreshortened—
Other men's children
can fall where they fall:

Other men's daughters
aren't that important
Other men's sons
don't matter at all.

Limber Climbers Clamber Up

The sky is full of stars
An astronomical number—
Limber climbers clamber up the slopes
In search of lumber
Lightning strikes the mountain path
From a solitary cloud
The quiet valley empties out
then fills again with thunder.

The Knife, Again

When those you say
You shouldn't have hurt
Show any sign of life, again,
Your hand goes for the knife, again.

Part of the Fun's Resisting

Part of the fun's resisting
Part of the fun's giving in
Part of the fun's life insisting that
we do it again and again.

Breeze May Moisten Wind May Whip

Breeze may moisten
Wind may whip
faces peering off a ship
crooked fingers grasp and grip
the ropes that burn like poison in the palms
the ropes that slacken
start to slip—

Sun may blacken
Sun may bleach
The broken branches on the beach
Bracken crabs commit their claws
To intermittent digging actions
Squat expansions
flat contractions

While heaping up extensions of their qualms
Gulls dive down and cross them out like bombs.

The Wonder of the Chrysalis

An ape
Leaving the trees
And losing its hair
Doesn't really compare.

I Don't See Me

I don't see me
As you see me
I don't see you
As you see you

Do you see how
You don't see you, or me
As I see me
And you?

You'll never see as others do—
How on earth do others see?
I guess it can't be shown to me
I guess it can't be shown to you

I can't know what's unknown to me
You can't know what's unknown to you—
These problems overblown by me
Are sure to be outgrown by you.

The Puzzled Toddler

Red sun in blue sky woke her
Suddenly up
on a porch of ochre

the puzzled toddler
ogled in awe
a muzzled pup raised a quizzical paw

yawning, yawning—lower the awning,
rain comes running
and jumping to soak her.

Needs Unmet

Too much to unravel
Too much to know
Too far to travel
Too late to go

Can you guess
Yes or no
If this is
Or isn't so?

Outermost outpost
Horse at the hitching post
Riding crop—chip-chop
Needs unmet

Two cars uncoupled
Two souls unwed
Two lives undone
Needs unmet

Outermost outpost
Underdone or overdosed
Come to a sliding stop
Needs unmet

To do
to be
To stop
to see
To try
to agree—
Fall on
your knee.

Don't fall
overboard
Don't strike
the wrong chord
Don't fall
on your sword
or
from a tree

Outermost outpost
Potato-gravy pot roast
Just another whistle stop
Needs unmet

You went second
I went first
You went forward
I reversed

Can you guess
More or less
Who I am
No or yes?

Outermost outpost
Silver on the gold coast
Hip hop beauty shop
Needs unmet.

The Skeleton and the Princess

The skeleton woke the princess up—
Saying, 'I need some skin.'
'First you need some muscle' she said.
'Look at the shape you're in!'

'All creaks and cracks
and yawning gaps
your ribs are like ribbons of shin.'

The skeleton moaned, the skeleton shook
the skeleton gave her a dirty look
and folded its boniness into a book
That the princess shut and locked with a hook
That somehow or other she later mistook
For a comb to her chagrin

A catacomb's
Not a comb for a cat
But a catacomb's
Not as bad as all that
The skeleton stood and the skeleton sat
then collapsed like a bowling pin
like a kitten's ear
or a crumpled bat.

In the Land of the Hooded Bubba

The dawn never came but the moon shone the same
In the land of the Hooded Bubba
The worms were white and they shone in the night
In the land of the Hooded Bubba

The wolves were black and they always came back
And the breeze never blew and no flowers grew
And I was just as lonely as you
In the land of the Hooded Bubba

While you knelt down to any old Crown
I knelt to the Hooded Bubba

You wished to impress
A young girl in a dress
And I, the Hooded Bubba
You came to confess
To a prim Priest-ess
And I, to the Hooded Bubba

The Hooded Bubba slept and slept
And all of his servants gathered and wept
Then finally, away they crept
From the land of the Hooded Bubba.

Now I alone, tonight, remain
The chance to leave won't come again
This empty land is my domain—
Till the end
of the Hooded Bubba.

Ender's Luck

If at the start
you're stuck:
you mean to blow
instead you suck

or strike a blow
then when it's struck
you stand
but have to duck—

If at the start
you suffer from
a change of heart
stop short

go numb
and fall apart—
misplace your pluck—
then if you're patient

if you're smart
you'll keep going as you are
there's a chance you'll still go far
if you count on ender's luck.

Important News

Chased by armed angels
Through the gates
Adam weeps.
But Eve, being shrewd,
Kept the seeds in her cheeks.

Sink

You're driven by desire
I'm drifting on a whim
You're heading for the centre
I'm clinging to the rim
You keep growing brighter
I keep going dim

You go I stop
You lift I drop
You stare I blink
We're out of sync

And when it's time to dive straight in
You won't need to stop to think
You'll dive in and swim and swim—
I'll slip off the edge and sink.

On the Value of Examining All Viewpoints

Someone's shifting buttocks:
The whole performance
From the viewpoint of the chairs.

He Just Happened, She Occurred

She implied, he inferred
She decided, he concurred
He was frightened, she was stirred
She got well, he was cured

She was voice, he was word
He encouraged, she deterred
He was tree, she was bird
She made obvious, he obscured

She objected, he observed
She subjected, he served
He upset, she unnerved
He just happened, she occurred.

Differences

One
acts as axle
the other acts as wheel.
The differences between
illusion and reality
are illusory and real.

The Hat

If you wear the hat after someone else
You think his thoughts
If someone wears it after you
She knows what you've been thinking

If nobody wears it for a long time
It starts to have thoughts of its own
Then nobody can wear it.

Don't Forget Yourself

You're not a lost sock at the laundromat
Or a book shelved on the wrong shelf
When others forget you
Of course it hurts—
But never forget yourself.

Found Wanting

You can't help wanting what you want—
wants come and go
in spite of you—
the problem isn't what you want
it's what you feel entitled to.

A Nanny in a Van

A nanny in a van
Drove a ninny to an Inn
The nanny from Dalwhinnie was as skinny as a pin
The ninny had a mini little midget for a granny—
As kin the granny's likeness to the nanny was uncanny.

Y Experiments

AY—Fantasy

Hazy day, hydrants spray
Angry tyrants stay away
Pyracantha calmly sways
Party cymbals, baby's play.

EY—Mystery keys

Enemy eyes everywhere
Myself: sleepy sentry
Pretty, velvety eyes
Gently deny entry.

IY—Hybrid idylls

Tipsy, giddy mystic
Visibly flying!
Finicky skinny ministry's
Tiny dignity dying ...

OY—Nobody's boy

Nobody's boy—
Nobody's rowdy,
Moody boy—
(Nobody's sorry).
Nobody's symbol—
Nobody's mythology
Nobody's story.

UY—Unlucky bully

Puny guy. Burly bully.
Burly bully's glumly bulky.
Puny guy: funny, funky.
Surly, burly bully's sulky.

The Few

The few needed some space
The many needed it too
But the many had to make do
With corners to rent from the few

A few needed reassurance
The many needed some too
But the many had to make do
With the scornful contempt of the few

A few needed time to think
The many needed some too
But the many had to make do
With a few moments left by the few

The few made a plan for the future
The many wanted to too
but the many got leftover futures
and a hand-me-down past from the few.

Bone-Idle Builders at a Barbecue

Bone-idle builders
and evil-deed doers

Dismal ditch-diggers
dredging the sewers

Scandalized witnesses
traumatized viewers

Hooks and enticements
temptations and lures

Baits and embellishments
shish kebab skewers

Salt

You find savour
in the salt
You find flavour,
I find fault.
On your mark,
get set—hold on—halt!
Hunker down, hurdle—
Giddy-up—vault!

Bearded Bob and Betty-Boo

Betty-Boo the waitress
forgets to bring the bill
She's hugging all her customers
which indicates goodwill

Big belted bearded Bob
waves his bag of chips
outside his rusted pickup truck—
the carburetor drips

Bearded Bob and Betty-Boo
Are people just like me and you
There's nothing here to misconstrue
There's nothing they do we don't do

That's all there is, that's it—adieu.

Up in Smoke

Ten more seconds
Up in smoke
There's a hitch
And there's a catch

Over the rainbow—
Down the hatch
Prickly thistles—
Bristling missiles—

Fissure in the eggshell
Crack the batch
You've got a fracture
Make it match

Look on the bright side
You're on the right side

Duck and hide, and
Lift the latch
A little more muscle to
Wind it back

Use your shoulder—
Take the slack
Retreat, stand still
Turn, attack.

Study the Sturdy

Study the sturdy
Avoid the insane
Be stable
like Abel
And watch out for Cain.

Two Vile Versifiers

for Michael Heyman

Two vile versifiers
walked into a bar—
one went almost nowhere,
the other went too far.

One pickled his epoch,
the other sliced it thin,
one had to hiccup—
the other had to grin.

One had a tunnel,
the other had a wall,
one feared collapse,
the other feared a fall.

One had a bomb on a belt above his bum,
the other kept a thimble as a symbol of his thumb.

Is It?

It is what it is
but it isn't
it never is

what it is
that's what you
say when you

don't know what
it is or
what to say

about it it's
fine to say
it but it

isn't okay to
say it isn't
what it is

if you don't
know what it
is is it

Dmitri in the Yew Tree

Dmitri in the yew tree
Had a country to conquer
Anatoly feeling holy
Grabbed Dmitri by the honker
Vladislav said all you have
Is some conniver by the nose
Little Zlata said you oughta
Let it go before it blows.

Annie Wong and Andy White

Annie Wong and Andy White
Saved the day
and spent the night
Gave away
grabbed and took
Snuggled
up into a cozy nook.

Happy Customer Number One

I give all answers
No questions asked

I can solve
personal problems
child mistakes
jealousy
depression
hair recession
I can solve
business
remove black magic
jadoo, hoodoo
no-good guru

Anointment with ointment
no need for appointment!

I can solve
enemies
immediate solution
witchcraft, divorce
eradicate
pollution

I can solve
Mississauga
or a barking dog a
hundred percent
satisfaction
no distraction
one hundred percent
protection
no deceit
completely discreet

no receipt
no detection

Call
master consultant
twenty-four hours
sleepless and efficient
adept and omniscient

I can solve
impossible problems!

Worries
with spirits
defective equipment
long-lost cargo
same day shipment

Opposite dollarama
above jeweller
next to highway
in pooja hut

Most powerful healer can handle
overpowering *over*-powers

can deal with love
and bring back the dead
fifty percent off!

no frills
and finish off
unloved ones
one generation to the next
always always
making you
our number one
happy customer

So

I don't believe it—
She knew what she was doing!
Eve was responsible
Adam said
So.

So—
Adam said
Eve was responsible?
She knew what she was doing?
I don't believe it.

Either Way ...

'Never,' said
God,
'Can special exceptions be made
For the commandment "Thou shalt not kill".'

For the commandment 'Thou shalt not kill'
Can special exceptions be made?
God
Never said.

Up and Down

At first sight
I truly loved you
Later
I wasn't so sure
I was good enough for you.

(I *was* good enough for you.
I wasn't so sure
Later
I truly loved you
At first sight.)

Either Way, Again

Noah
Saved
The animals
On the ark—
Noah
Fed
The animals
Fed
Noah
On the ark—
The animals
Saved
Noah.

Witness the Wetness

Witness the wetness
The witless will wonder
Why you're walking in the rain
By thunder?
To some it's nothing
But to others it's frightening
when their windswept footsteps
are followed by lightning.

What Lessons Have You Learned?

What lessons have you learned from the resolve of
    captive nations?
From greed, from need, from noble deeds—from life's
    humiliations?
From fielding barbs at barbecues
amongst your close relations?

I learned to dance in paisley pants
to laugh and snap a string
In other words my little birds,
I haven't learned a thing.

Philosophers Assist Her with the Loss of Her Lucifer

The loss of her Lucifer troubled her
Philosophers tried to assist
They told her that none would think less of her
That the least of her troubles was this—
Was this loss of her lost-to-her Lucifer ...
That she'd not seen the last of this Lucifer ...
that there'd soon be a great deal more news of her
once they'd set her old Lucifer loose in her.

Open Fire

They sat around an open fire—
somebody shouted
'Open fire!'
Shots rang out and the flames leapt higher

What the—!
sang the heavenly choir
as the flames ripped through
their angelic attire.

A Hand to Hold

Instead of a dreadful headful
Give us some warmth in the cold
give us a cheerful earful
show us your heart of gold.
Instead of a harmful armful
Give us a hand to hold.

The Self I Couldn't Find

My dreams remembered
how I was designed—
They broke back into my body
through my mind and helped
me find the self
I couldn't find.

Dropping a Knot

Illuminate the loop in it
Eliminate the loop
Elucidate and loosen it
And if it falls
down you swoop—
Tighten it
beware the knot
if it drops
you might
have to stoop
to pick it up
You mustn't stop
to convalesce
nevertheless
the scoop
is that there's always time
to slow down—
drop your thoughts off
close your eyelids
give up your undecideds

take a deep breath
and recoup.

The Matter of Facts

Were you certain because you were right?
I was sure even though I was wrong!
Are we sure now which facts we weren't sure
or were sure of were facts or weren't facts all along?

Wolf Pack

Great Lakes bunch back like the backs
Of a wolf pack
Their heads sunk in the sand
Their tails under the banks

All you see of them
Is what
They've turned to you—
Their backs—

While their wolf bellies drag
Shallow fish-paths
And brush rusted hulls
Little people pit their edges

With buckets and blankets
Little people build their cities
And drain their sorrows into
Gitchi-gami Mishigami Karegnondi

Erielhonan Onitariio
Out they go
Filling their hopes
In the rapids

In the narrows
Down the
Kaniatarowanenneh
Into the great gta'n

Lotta Things Gotta Go

Lotta things
Gotta go
Gasoline
Spring snow
Now you see it
Now you know
Lotta things
Oughta go

Gotta stop
Losing track
Gonna give it
All back
Full hole
Empty crack
Gotta stop
Looking back

Getta grip
Let go
Gonna trip
Although
Lotta things
Start to settle
Cold fire
Under kettle

Gonna getcha
In the end
And you know it
But pretend
That you're gonna
Live forever
Pretty clueless
Stupid/clever

Gotcha going
Gotcha back
Jane Doe
Mary Mack
Gotta know
Gotta knack
Eyes flow
Ice pack

Humdrum Hubbub

Humdrum hubbub
restful ruckus
Timid tumult
luck may pluck us
From a self-induced disaster
but good sense
will do it faster.

Your Livelihood

Be lively about
Your livelihood
Before what's good
Is gone for good.

Have Bits or All

Have bits or all of either of these
Have half of all the rest
Call it quits whenever you please
Be gone now be my guest.

Do Do-Gooders Do

Do do-gooders do
what's truly good?
Do well-wishers wish us
as well as they should?
Do browbeaters bring us
what wise counsel could?
You'll understand
once you've understood.

What Awaits Us

What awaits us
In the oasis?
Frantic scrambles
Or a time of stasis?

The Day That's Ended

There's nothing quite
Like the day that's ended
No one knows
If the next one's coming—
The room goes dark and the rain starts drumming
The wind is high, but not like a tower
There's nothing quite
Like the day's last hour.

Nine Extra Thoughts (No Extra Cost)

Why, at this point, would anyone want to make history? Humans have been making history for 10,000 years—the time has come to make something else.

A bird-watching word butcher is both word botcher and bird watcher.

The problem troubled people most often face is recognizing when there isn't a problem.

If talking stops working stop talking.

If you're really beyond it, there's no reason to behave as if you're above it.

Now when I look back I wonder why I ever looked back.

If you can't join them, judge them.

It's easy to see through people, much harder to look carefully into them.

How can people live with themselves when they know that they have to die with themselves?

Before cutting anyone down to size, make sure that you measure them carefully.

How I Like Them

I like how they sit back
to think and lean forward
to talk

I like how alike
they are and how different
I like how they exaggerate their pursuit of clarity

And at other times in other places
clarify their exaggerations
I like how details distract them

but rarely the bigger picture
I like the subtle successes they pass on
quietly to their successors

And their clumsy attempts that become
their culture
Look how they celebrate one another

You have to like that
And the richness of their dreams
And it's hard not to love

their love of invention
And their expressions
in their words

and on their faces
observing their friendships
in beautiful moments

and across hard decades I can't help it
I look at them I look at them
And I like them.

At the End of the World

In come the oceans
Out go the mountains
Volcanoes erupting
Like soda pop fountains

Souls of our ancestors
Rose up and swirled
To watch from the moon
At the end of the world.

Acknowledgements

Different (or identical) versions of a few of these appeared first in *Love is an Observant Traveller, Inklings, Taddle Creek, Bookbird, Quadrant* (Australia) and *There Devil, Eat That*. My attempt at the reverso format in several poems was inspired by the incomparable example set by Marilyn Singer in her remarkable *Mirror Mirror: A Book of Reverso Poems*. Thank you to the Ontario Arts Council's Writer's Reserve Program, Conan Tobias (*Taddle Creek*), Les Murray (*Quadrant*), Beth Follett (Pedlar Press), Barry Callaghan (Exile Editions), Paul Lisson and Fiona Kinsella (Hamilton Arts and Letters), Björn Sundmark and Michael Heyman (*Bookbird*).

I can't thank Tim and Elke Inkster and Stephanie Small enough for all of their support and good advice in the making of this book. And Chandra Wohleber for her helpful suggestions.

I'm deeply indebted to Alec Dempster for the dark beauty and humour of his artwork.

Thank you to Frank Kelley, president of the Hobo Foundation in Britt, Iowa, for responding reassuringly to concerns my family had about the book's title.

And where would I be without my dear family? Amy, Sophie, Ashey and JoJo—you make everything fun and interesting and worthwhile in the simplest way by just being yourselves.

About the Author

Born in Hamilton, Ontario, and raised nearby in Dundas, JonArno Lawson is a four-time winner of the Lion and the Unicorn Award for Excellence in North American Children's Poetry: in 2007 for *Black Stars in a White Night Sky*, in 2009 for *A Voweller's Bestiary*, in 2013 for *Down in the Bottom of the Bottom of the Box* and in 2014 for *Enjoy It While It Hurts*. In 2011 his poetry collection *Think Again* was shortlisted for the Ruth and Sylvia Schwartz Children's Book Award. *Sidewalk Flowers* won the Governor General's Award for Illustrated Children's Books in 2015. JonArno lives in Toronto with his wife, Amy Freedman, and his children Sophie, Ashey and Joseph, all of whom assist the author with phrases, topics and sometimes even complete lines for use in his poems.

About the Illustrator

Alec Dempster was born in Mexico City but as a child moved with his family to Toronto. He later returned to Mexico and settled in Xalapa, Veracruz, where his relief prints eventually became infused with the local tradition of son jarocho music. He has produced six CDs of son jarocho and has presented solo exhibitions of his prints throughout the world. He is also the author of two books documenting traditional Mexican art, music and dance: *Lotería Jarocha* (2013) and *Lotería Huasteca* (2015). Alec lives in Toronto.